TO

....

FROM

....

DATE

....

Hope *and* Comfort *for* Every Season

Cecil Murphey

PHOTOGRAPHY BY NANCY J. LOCKE

HARVEST HOUSE PUBLISHERS

EUGENE, OREGON

HOPE AND COMFORT FOR EVERY SEASON
Text Copyright © 2010 by Cecil Murphey
Artwork © Nancy J. Locke, LLC

Published by Harvest House Publishers
Eugene, Oregon 97402
www.harvesthousepublishers.com

ISBN 978-0-7369-2607-2

Cover photo: Tahquamenon Falls State Park, Michigan.

All photographs taken in Michigan, including: Porcupine Mountains Wilderness,
Tahquamenon Falls and Van Riper State Parks, Hiawatha and Ottawa National Forests,
Pictured Rocks National Lakeshore, Lakes Huron and Superior, and the photographer's land.

Design and production by Koechel Peterson and Associates, Minneapolis, Minnesota

All Scripture quotations are from the *Holy Bible*, New Living Translation, copyright ©1996,
2004. Used by permission of Tyndale House Publishers, Inc., Wheaton, IL 60189 USA. All
rights reserved.

Printed in China

10 11 12 13 14 15 16 / **LP** / 10 9 8 7 6 5 4 3 2

CONTENTS

For everything there is a season,
a time for every activity under heaven.

ECCLESIASTES 3:1

CHOOSING THE SEASONS

TODAY HAS BEEN A DIFFICULT DAY. I feel discouraged. That's strange because two days ago I thought about how much I enjoyed my life and decided I wouldn't have it any other way.

Maybe that's the problem: *I wouldn't have it any other way.* I wanted my life to remain forever on that delightful, calm level—to stay the way it is when I feel happy and life goes smoothly.

But life doesn't function like that. "For everything there is a season, a time for every activity under heaven," the wise man wrote in the book of Ecclesiastes.

Even though I know that, I hear myself asking, "But why the bad times now?" As I ask myself that question, I start to laugh. "When would be the convenient time?"

"For everything there is a season," the wise man's words remind me.

I nod and agree. Maybe I could enjoy those times if I could choose when they happen. Again I laugh at myself. The seasons are inevitable and beyond my control. They're in God's hands.

Too often I forget. I prepare for life to open up in one particular direction and later realize I've followed a dead-end road.

I want control of my life so I can experience more joy and a sense of well-being in the happy seasons.

During the painful seasons, I want to experience less (actually none) of the pain and heartache.

Instead of attempting to control what I can't, perhaps I can learn to let go of my plans and say, "Thank You, God, for choosing this season for me."

Ever-wise and ever-loving God, thank You for not letting me choose the seasons. If I had the choice, I'd learn only the easy lessons. Remind me that there are difficult and painful things I need for my growth. You know what I need long before I figure it out. You choose so that I'll become more Christlike and loving. Amen.

Today is a new day. Today I can be different.

A time to be born and a time to die.
A time to plant and a time to harvest.

ECCLESIASTES 3:2

PREPARING AND RECEIVING

IN 2007 OUR HOUSE BURNED, and we lost everything we'd accumulated through the years. But we lost something more valuable than property. Our son-in-law, Alan, died in the fire. We can always replace things; we can't replace those we love.

Shirley and our daughter, Cecile, stayed on a neighbor's lawn on the right side of the house and hardly moved until the firefighters left.

Suffering itself has no value. Value lies in the lessons I learn from suffering.

I was on the opposite side of the driveway. I stood alone and needed to be alone. As I assessed the loss and grieved for the son-in-law I loved, a deep sense of peace and an awareness of God's presence filled my heart. In those moments I thought of the biblical story of Job and his losses. "Who am I to think I should be immune?" I said aloud.

Shirley said little, but her attitude was amazingly similar to mine. We grieved for Alan, but we didn't fall apart, scream at God, or wonder why God punished us.

For several days after the fire, our children hovered around us; friends came to embrace and encourage us; neighbors shared clothing and other items. Several people commented on how well Shirley and I handled the tragedy.

A neighbor asked, "How can you be so calm?"

For several seconds I stared at him and finally said, "I've been preparing for this loss."

I didn't mean I saw it coming, but God had taken Shirley and me through tragedies and losses, heartache and disappointments. At the time a few of them devastated us, but we eventually put them behind us. When this tragedy struck, God had prepared us so that we could handle the loss. Now we were able to accept this tragedy and to thank God for always being with us, even in the darkest moments.

Shirley and I aren't unique. One of the advantages of aging is that we mature and no longer expect total happiness and life without hardship. We learn the seasons of life by living with and trusting in a God who loves us.

It's not that our lives have been worse than those of others—they haven't. They have been *different* and that's the way God works in us. Each trial and every hardship strengthens us to face the next disappointment. To accept that life works that way doesn't make death or serious illness easy, but it reminds us that both are part of life.

In the words of a wise man, there is a time to be born and a time to die. In typical Hebraic poetic style, he repeats the idea using different words. He moves from human experience to nature. There is a time to plant seeds and there is a time for the harvest. That's another way to show the cycle of life. He writes not only of birth and of death, he also writes of planting and harvesting. That's the same message twice.

We sow our crops and seek a bountiful harvest. If conditions are good, when the time of harvest comes, we pull the tomatoes from the plants and cut the lettuce leaves. Once they've borne their fruit, the plants die. It's the end of their season.

At times, however, we seem to reap nothing but disappointment and dissatisfaction. If we're honest, we admit that we sowed the wrong kind of seed or sowed it in the wrong place. We may have planned for personal satisfaction and neglected other things in our lives— our families, our church, our marriage.

My emotions are only feelings; my emotions are not reality. I may feel like a failure but that doesn't make me a failure.

We need to remind ourselves that the present is the result of past experiences. We plant for the future right now, and perhaps we need to pause and examine what we're doing. We may need to plow up the old crops. We may need to ponder the poor quality of our sowing. Or to rethink our attitudes, motives, and feelings toward others. We may need to bring to the surface painful memories that we have plowed under. If we face our resentments, anger, mistakes, and prejudices, we can pull them from our lives and begin to plant with new seeds.

That's how life works: We move from birth to death, from sowing to reaping. We can't pick the seasons or the events, but we can determine what we sow by our attitude. If we choose well, we'll be amply rewarded at the time of harvest.

As we near the end of life, we can look back and remember the loss of friendships, termination of jobs or careers, times of better health, and other things we've left behind. We can focus on those things taken from us or we can realize that loss can also bring freedom. We shed the burdens of earlier years and move on. We can smile as we think of our newfound freedom. We don't have to worry about how people perceive us. We don't have to fit into a pattern of behavior that our former roles demanded.

The best gift is the freedom from the tyranny of time. After years of keeping set hours for work and leisure, regulated mealtimes, stated bedtimes, we can create new patterns for our lives.

We have time to talk. We have time to listen. We have opportunities to read, to explore, and to think new thoughts. God planned the seasons and they are for us to enjoy.

A time to kill and a time to heal.
A time to tear down and a time to build up.

ECCLESIASTES 3:3

FROM OLD ENDINGS
TO NEW BEGINNINGS

I HAD TO BREAK OFF my friendship with Gloria," Alice said. "I've known her for twenty years, but I couldn't take any more."

It was a sad time for Alice even though she did the right thing. She could have said, "It was time to kill the friendship." I understood the situation, but I sat quietly and let her talk.

"I tried to be her friend, but she's negative about everything. Nothing suits her. I wanted to see her enjoy life. I tried to talk positively to her.

She read the books I gave her and listened to the CDs, but nothing changed."

One time I overheard Gloria say to Alice, "If your life was half as hard as mine, you'd feel as pessimistic as I do."

I didn't intervene, but the issue wasn't whose life was more difficult. The issue was about a negative attitude. Gloria herself killed many relationships because she focused only on her own misery.

Most of us don't kill relationships easily. *To kill* a relationship sounds harsh. But a time to kill may mean destroying a bad relationship and distancing yourself from that person. It may mean leaving a job you've had for years. It can be the death of a relationship as it existed, and you work for healing so that it becomes new. What you need to slaughter isn't as important as facing the reality that some things must come to an end.

I have three children, whom I love very much. While they were growing up, I tried my best to impart my values and my beliefs. They're now grown and have children of their own. Over the years, we terminated the daddy–young child connection. These days they treat me like an adult, and I like that. From my perspective, they're now my friends—my younger friends—and I feel our connectedness is even stronger. As I do with any adult friends, I offer advice only when they ask. If we think of killing as a violent act, perhaps it's easier to focus on the parallel words of the wise writer. He talks about tearing down and rebuilding.

I can make today and every day the best season of my life. My attitude determines what's good and what's bad.

We learn to overcome negativity by avoiding those who spread such a spirit. We can also remind ourselves that the positive can overcome the negative. Good can triumph over evil.

Someone urged me to smile at adversity. I've not been able to do that, but I've learned to eliminate bad emotions quickly. I choose not to hold on to them or allow them to control my thinking and my actions. Adversity is part of life, but we can learn to be grateful for difficult times because they force us to grow and to expand our capacity. Human character isn't formed by the absence of hardship but by our responses to the turmoil.

§

We can't start the new until we get rid of the old. Too many of us want to hold on to the old way of life—old associations, former jobs, the places we used to live.

Perhaps we try to hold on to our image as youthful and energetic. As long as we stay emotionally attached to the former, we're not ready to enjoy the new adventure. We can't rebuild until we've torn down.

Tearing down can be painful, but when we look back (and it may take years), we can say to ourselves, "It was right to tear it down so I could build the new."

Life won't go smoothly, and we must constantly tear down and rebuild. Tragedy and heartache seem to come to us as suddenly as a storm. But we can rise above the storms.

When we lived in Kenya, I liked to observe the coconut trees during the monsoon season. Torrential rains and heavy winds ravaged the land, and the coconut palms bent—sometimes parallel to the ground—and stayed there as if to duck the storms. Because they could bend, they didn't break.

That's just as true with us: If we can bend, we can survive. We bend when we accept that this is how life works. If we shake our fists at adversity, we break.

Welcoming the new doesn't always mean destroying or abandoning the old, but it does mean things must change. Sometimes we like to keep old and trusted friends and maintain family ties. But over the years the relationships must become new in order to remain significant.

Our relationship with God changes. When I first became a believer I saw God as the One who protected me from evil and who provided for my needs. That's still true. But as I grew, I put to death that limited understanding. I've learned to enjoy the divine companionship and to think of Jesus as a brother and someone who walks through life with His hand on my shoulder. Like a child who has grown up, I ask for fewer things but desire more contact.

Too often, however, we kill relationships that we truly need to preserve. We kill them by neglect, by not answering letters or emails or returning phone calls. If we ignore the needs and the feelings of others, we kill those relationships.

We may reach the success we yearned to reach, but we need to ask ourselves, "Was it worth it?" If we neglect our relationship with God, we'll already know the answer.

God, sometimes it's comfortable to follow the same roads day after day, even if they're not healthy paths. Help me know when it's time to slay parts of my past so I can be open to the future. Amen.

A time to cry and a time to laugh.
A time to grieve and a time to dance.

ECCLESIASTES 3:4

CRYING AND LAUGHING

I LEARNED SOMETHING after the death of my brother Mel. After the funeral we gathered in the church basement for sandwiches and dessert. We walked into the building with sad faces. Within minutes, someone behind me giggled and another person laughed aloud. A group of six or seven of his friends regaled each other with stories of Mel's little jokes and fun times.

At every age I want to grow, search, and discover the truth about myself, about God, and about my world.

"He could tell even a stupid joke, and I'd laugh at the way he told it," one man said.

Tears filled my eyes. I wouldn't ever see Mel or listen to his jokes again.

Just then I realized that the two extreme emotions are closer than we think. As kids we often cried one minute and laughed and played the next.

Perhaps the difference is that when we're adults, it takes us a little longer to shift our feelings. Children don't have any problem rushing from one emotion to another.

One summer morning Juanita told me she had fought with Doris. "I'll never speak to her again as long as I live." They were both in second grade, lived two blocks apart, and had been best friends. Three hours later, the two girls played together. When I reminded Juanita of what she had said, she laughed. "That was this morning."

Maybe some of us older people need to learn to change our emotions that quickly. Perhaps it helps if we remember the words from the Bible: "Get rid of all bitterness, rage, anger, harsh words, and slander, as well as all types of evil behavior. Instead, be kind to each other, tenderhearted, forgiving one another, just as God through Christ has forgiven you" (Ephesians 4:31-32).

I look like this because it's the face I've earned from my days on earth. Each day my face declares who I am before I say a word.

The wise writer also contrasts grief with dancing. We tend to think of grief as quiet and inward. And it can be. But in other cultures, grief entails wailing and crying aloud. By contrast, to dance is to express joy and happiness. I love to watch happy children. They dance uninhibited. I think that's how King David danced when the people brought the Ark of the Covenant back to Israel after it had been held by the Philistines.

"And David danced before the LORD with all his might... So David and all the people of Israel brought up the Ark of the LORD with shouts of joy and the blowing of rams' horns" (2 Samuel 6:14-15).

This reminds us that it's all right to feel. We need to allow ourselves to mourn or to rejoice, to dance or to scream out in pain.

We can also remind ourselves that grief doesn't last forever. Over time, the pain diminishes. Joy doesn't last either, so let's enjoy it when we feel it.

A time to scatter stones and a time to gather stones.
A time to embrace and a time to turn away.

SCATTERING AND GATHERING

WHEN SHIRLEY AND I LEFT FOR AFRICA, we had a time of embracing. We and our three children said our farewell to Shirley's mother and to Shirley's sister and her husband.

Just before I pulled out of the driveway, I looked back. Mom Brackett stood at the front door, tears in her eyes, and waved goodbye. Before we were out of sight, she turned away and closed the door behind her.

That's an example of how life works. We embrace those we care about, but we can't hold on to them. Eventually they travel their way, and we must go ours. Whether it's friendship, a parent-child relationship, or leaving to take a new job, at least one person eventually turns away.

I've noticed turning away at funerals. The tears flow among the family and friends, but the most painful moment seems to be at the gravesite. When the people get up to leave, some do so with reluctance, as if they want to prolong the moment. They start to leave, pause, turn back, and gaze for the last time at the casket. Others walk rapidly away and avoid even a backward glance.

As I think of the other part of the wise man's statement about gathering and scattering stones, I'm reminded of the time that our house burned to the ground and we had only partial walls and the

foundation left. Weeks later, a Cater-
pillar tore down the rest of the walls.
Large trucks carried away what had
become debris. A few months later, I
stood in the driveway and watched the
builders rebuild the walls.

That's the way life works. We seem
always to be tearing down or building.
Life and relationships never become
static. Something constantly changes.
We grow out of old relationships, and
we form new ones.

*Because God
is active in
the world, my
appreciation
of life can
improve.*

In the midst of gathering or embracing, we can give thanks and appreciate
what we have. Or we can mourn and
focus on what we don't have. Those
achievements, possessions, business deals,
or trophies don't make us happier.

As someone said, "Happiness is an inside job." It's an interior decision.

Our gathering is temporary as the words of the wise man imply. We gather, but we also scatter. We collect, but we also must give up. At the end, we take nothing with us; however, we can live in peace if we focus on what we leave behind. We can leave people happier and kinder. We can be those who help and encourage others to enjoy what they gather from their labors. It's a habit we can learn.

A decade ago I started a new practice. Each morning I recounted five things for which I was thankful. I ticked them off one by one. After a few weeks I decided to increase the number to ten. Now, after I reach ten, I stop counting but I don't stop being thankful. As a result, my stress level has decreased and I enjoy my life more.

But there's something more than being thankful that helps me. When I pause to thank God, I remind myself that my life is in His hands. The seasons that come and go are part of a loving Father's divine plan for life. The more I thank God for the good things, the more aware I am of His intervention.

As we learn to receive whatever life holds for us and give thanks, even praising God during the bad periods, we see life more clearly and objectively. We also realize that we are not the center of the world, but we are the center of God's love.

God of all seasons, remind me that this is life. We build and we tear down; we embrace and we turn away. Everything and everyone changes except You. May our biggest change be to accept a stronger, fuller embrace of Your love. Amen.

A time to search and a time to quit searching.
A time to keep and a time to throw away.

WE KEEP AND WE THROW AWAY

Most of us search for meaning and explanations about why things happen. We don't understand the difficult times as they occur. With the perspective of hindsight, we often look back and thank God for what seemed the worst of times. Or as one philosopher put it, "Life can only be understood backward; but it must be lived forward."

In our search for meaning, we also lose—or let go of—old things. We keep relics from our school days and eventually we decide to throw them away. I kept my major papers from college and grad school days.

The past will always be the past and I can't change it. But I can make decisions that will change the future.

Twenty years later, I looked at them and thought of the space they took up in my filing cabinet. "I haven't looked at them once since graduation," I told my wife. That day I threw them into the garbage.

But I kept one thing from that era. For ten Monday evenings, the late writer Charlie Shedd taught a course on writing for publication. At the final class, he handed me a letter written in green ink. Here is the important part: "You have a rare talent. If you continue to improve, in twenty-five years I'll be able to say, 'I knew you when.'"

I chose to keep that letter.

Why discard some things and hold on to others? The difference lies in the meaning of what we keep and what we throw away. When something is no longer useful, most of us discard it.

I had worked hard for my grades in school and the stored papers were the result. They represented my achievement, something I had earned.

Charlie's letter was different. I hadn't written to receive his praise. But that one page of fifty-three words encouraged me then. Over the next decade those words reminded me that I could continue to improve.

My school work was important, but Charlie's letter came as a surprise and gave me the courage to focus on a different direction for my life.

Most of us need those little things that build us up. But more than that, when we begin to waver, want to give up or throw away what we've worked for, those little things whisper, "Keep on. Keep on."

A time to tear and a time to mend.
A time to be quiet and a time to speak.

ECCLESIASTES 3:7

SILENCE AND SPEAKING

JIM KEILLER ASKED ME TO TEACH a few courses at a local Bible college, and the opportunity excited me. I had the credentials, knew the material, and felt I could do an adequate job.

Jim mailed me a doctrinal statement that I had to sign before I could teach. I disagreed with one item near the bottom of the page. It was one of those theological issues over which many Bible believers differ, but the document expressed the school's strong position on the matter.

Should I sign it? Refuse to sign it? I didn't know how to handle the situation.

Sometimes we don't speak up because it's easier than facing opposition or ridicule or being rejected. In this case, the issue might have been serious enough for them to say no to me. Was it a time when I should speak up?

I went to see Jim and explained the situation. "What should I do?" I asked. "I don't want to lie."

He told me to write one paragraph at the bottom of the page explaining my disagreement. I did. That was it; the school hired me.

Life doesn't always work like that. Sometimes to speak up causes factions and divisions. One time I was at a Christian conference, and a woman came to our small group late. She had been listening to a presidential debate. She apologized for being late, smiled, and said, "But our man is winning."

I didn't want to be viewed as an automatic supporter of a particular political party—especially one with whom I disagreed. "Who is *our man?*" I asked.

"If you don't know, you probably shouldn't be at this conference."

I said nothing more, but she sat next to me (the only empty chair left) and turned her chair so that I saw more of her back than her face. She didn't speak to me again. It saddened me that she was so convinced her political position was correct and, by implication, to disagree was to be wrong.

None of us are who we used to be; all of us are who we're becoming.

At other times, however, I've kept silent because the issue didn't seem significant. In those instances silence is sometimes wiser than speaking.

As the wise writer says, there is "a time to tear and a time to mend."

One factor in growing older is being able to sense when to speak and when to be silent. We often call that wisdom. Being older and being wise aren't the same. The wise are those who have lived and *learned* from their painful experiences. Wisdom reflects the character of the person who sees life with a healthy perspective, makes sensible decisions, and faces crises positively.

If we learn from the wise writer, we make this a time for examining and pondering. We reevaluate our lives and become less judgmental and more understanding. We're no longer upset over the things that once ruined an entire day. We become more open with ourselves and sincere with others. We realize not only that we live among imperfect people, but we're part of the imperfect people.

We don't have to feel wise to be wise, and it may be healthy to say, "I don't know." When we're honest about our lack of wisdom, our words may be extremely wise.

God of all words, help me know when to speak up and when to remain silent. Help me know when to dissolve relationships and when to seek reconciliation. I don't always know, but You do, so I want to rely on Your help. Amen.

A time to love and a time to hate.
A time for war and a time for peace.

ECCLESIASTES 3:8

LOVE AND HATE?

"WHY DO YOU HATE ME SO MUCH?" our daughter Wanda asked me.

"I don't hate you. I love you very much—"

"You pick on me all the time."

She was eight years old, and I knelt beside her and wrapped my arm around her shoulders. "It may seem like hate right now, but it's really a form of love." Before she could argue—and she was the child who would—I said, "You're older and more responsible than your sister and brother. I expect more from you."

I don't know if she understood, but I spoke to her for several minutes to assure her that I loved her. She had misbehaved, and it was more serious than if her younger sister or brother had done the same thing.

As I reflect on that incident, it makes me aware that most of us are a little like Wanda. We focus on what we want and not what's wise or best. We feel like screaming, "God, why do You hate me? Why are You punishing me?"

I saw this in a writer-friend a decade ago. She received rejection after rejection. One day she received a phone call from an editor. "We're interested in publishing your book, but we have a few questions." My friend answered the questions, and the conversation seemed to go well.

Six days later, she received an email in which the editor said they had decided not to publish her book. My friend called me and yelled about injustice and

God being against her.

She never published that book, despite her declarations that it was "extremely well written." To her credit, she started a new one in a different genre. Three years later she finally received a book contract. She called to tell me her good news.

"So you've made peace with God, have you?" I asked.

When I reminded her of the earlier conversation, she laughed. "That's how I felt then. I'm glad now that I didn't get the first book published," she added a bit sheepishly. "It wasn't very good."

Perhaps what seems like war or hatred from God may be love in disguise.

We can see others as flawed or we can see them as people much like ourselves.

It may be God's way of saying, "This thing you want isn't for you. I have something else planned for you."

At times, all of us are at war with God. It may not be fire-hot rebellion; it may be simply ignoring the right thing to do. It may be the reluctance to obey out of fear or uncertainty; it may be the inability to say to someone, "I was wrong. Please forgive me."

Whatever the form of war between God and us, a good way to seek peace is to pray, "God, I'm sorry for…"

Always-loving God, remind me that even the keenest disappointments aren't evidence that You stand against me. Instead, those times may be when You're closest and want me to change directions in my life. Help me to realize that when You withhold, You withhold out of love. I forget so easily, so remind me frequently. Amen.

THE SEASONS OF LIFE

TODAY I STARED AT MY FACE IN THE MIRROR. "Where did all those wrinkles come from?" I asked my image, and we both laughed.

"I've earned them," I said. "I've earned every one." And we all do.

Years ago a woman named Pauline was a member of the congregation where I pastored. I tried to be friendly, but it didn't seem to work with her.

What I remember most about her appearance was the downturned mouth. Even when she smiled (which was rare), she couldn't hide that.

At the time I prayed, "God, when I'm as old as Pauline, help me have upturned lips." I wanted to live in such a way that when I reached an advanced age, my face would show my attitude and lifestyle without my having to say a word.

In my book, *Aging Is an Attitude*, I started a chapter with these words: "The face you have at age twenty is the one you were born with. Your face at age forty is who you are becoming. Your face at age sixty is the face you deserve."

When Shirley and I were in our twenties, she would often say about an older person, "Look at his laugh wrinkles." That was her way of saying that he or she looked like a happy person.

God has determined the seasons and the times of life. Only God knows what lies ahead, just as He knew our past before it happened. *God decides the seasons; we choose the response.* We can rejoice that God loves us enough to send the hardships and holds our hands and dries our tears to take us through those hard places.

On the other side of each trial, we can look back, smile at loved ones behind us, and say, "Take my hand. I've already been over that part of the road, and I can guide you part of the way."

There truly is a time for everything under heaven. And we need to be aware that we need every one of those seasons.

Each day we can learn to say, "Thank You, God, for the seasons of my life."

We need seasons to mature us, to become who we're supposed to be to fulfill God's loving, gracious plan for our lives. Along the way ambitions change and our horizons shrink.

§

Powerful forces constantly work within us. It's as if winds of adversity afflict us one moment, and sunshine warms us the next. Our attitude determines our behavior as well as our preparation for the next weather change.

We can react negatively and wail, "Life is only a one-way street that ends in death." True, it does. But there's more to the good life than living on the one-way street. We can remind ourselves, "This is life right now, and I have my share of problems and heartaches. God never promised me personal immunity."